Life Cyc

:k

sbury

www.raintreepublishers.co.uk
Visit our website to find out more information about **Raintree** books.

To order:
☎ Phone 44 (0) 1865 888112
▤ Send a fax to 44 (0) 1865 314091
▢ Visit the Raintree Bookshop at **raintreepublishers.co.uk** to browse our catalogue and order online.

First published in Great Britain by Raintree, Halley Court, Jordan Hill, Oxford OX2 8EJ, part of Harcourt Education.
Heinemann is a registered trademark of Harcourt Education Ltd.

© Harcourt Education Ltd 2003
First published in paperback in 2004
The moral right of the proprietor has been asserted.

Editorial: Charlotte Guillain and Diyan Leake
Design: Michelle Lisseter
Picture Research: Maria Joannou and Debra Weatherley
Production: Lorraine Hicks

Originated by Dot Gradations
Printed and bound in China by South China Printing Company

ISBN 1 844 21248 3 (hardback)
07 06 05 04
10 9 8 7 6 5 4 3 2

ISBN 1 844 21253 X (paperback)
08 07 06 05 04
10 9 8 7 6 5 4 3 2 1

British Library Cataloguing in Publication Data
Spilsbury, Louise
Duck
571.8'1841
A full catalogue record for this book is available from the British Library.

Acknowledgements
The publishers would like to thank the following for permission to reproduce photographs: Alamy Images pp. **6**, **22**, **23** (beak); Ardea (John Daniels) pp. **5**, **16**; Bruce Coleman pp. **13** (Jane Burton), **17** (Jane Burton), **21** (Tero Niemi), **23** (webbed feet, Jane Burton; wings, Tero Niemi), back cover (duckling, Jane Burton); Corbis (George D. Lepp) p. **15**; FLPA (D. Hosking) p. **14**; Getty Images (Imagebank) p. **20**; Nature Picture Library pp. **7** (Tom Vezo), **9** (Steven D. Miller), **12** (Mike Wilkes), **19** (Pete Oxford), back cover (eggs, Steven D. Miller); NHPA (Bill Coster) p. **8**; Oxford Scientific Films pp. **4** (Martyn Chillmaid), **10** (Joaquin Gutierrez Acha), **23** (lay, Joaquin Gutierrez Acha); Papilio p. **11** (Robert Pickett); Science Photo Library (Bill Bachman/ Photo Researchers) p. **18**

Cover photograph of a duck, reproduced with permission of Corbis (Lynda Richardson)

Every effort has been made to contact copyright holders of any material reproduced in this book. Any omissions will be rectified in subsequent printings if notice is given to the publishers.

Contents

Some words are shown in bold, **like this**. They are explained in the glossary on page 23.

What are ducks?

These are ducks.

Ducks are birds that like to live near water.

Birds start life inside an egg.

When do ducks lay eggs?

Mother ducks **lay** eggs in spring.

They lay the eggs in a nest.

This mother duck has brown feathers.

This father duck has green feathers on his head and neck.

What are nests like?

The mother duck makes a nest from leaves and grass.

The father duck chases other ducks away from it.

The mother duck puts soft plants inside the nest.

Then she **lays** her eggs in the nest.

Who looks after the eggs?

The mother duck sits on the eggs to keep them warm.

This helps the babies inside to grow.

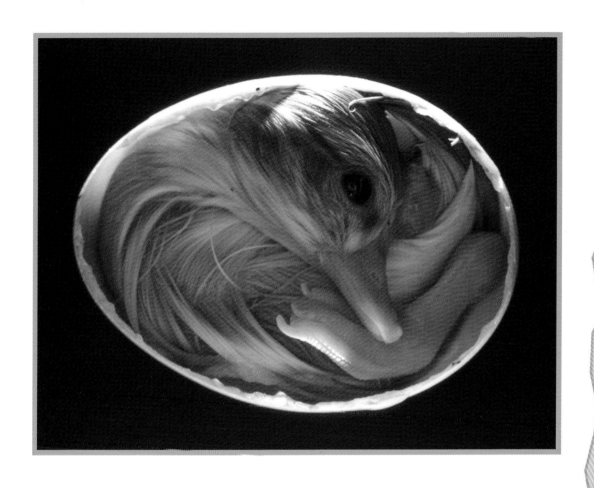

This picture shows the inside of an egg.

The baby duck is ready to come out.

How do baby birds get out of the eggs?

After a month the baby ducks come out of the eggs.

They break open the egg with their **beaks**.

Baby ducks are called ducklings.

They are covered in soft fluffy feathers called down.

When do ducklings leave the nest?

The new ducklings are very hungry.

They leave the nest to find food right away.

The ducklings follow their mother to find food.

They swim behind her in a line.

What do ducks eat?

The mother duck shows the ducklings what to eat.

She dips her head underwater and eats plants.

Ducks have **webbed feet**.

Webbed feet help them swim
and dive to get food.

How do ducklings keep safe?

Big birds and fish try to eat ducklings.

The mother duck calls the ducklings to come to her.

Ducklings stay close to their mother.

She keeps them safe under her **wings**.

When do ducklings learn to fly?

Ducklings learn to fly when they are six weeks old.

They flap their **wings** to fly.

When ducklings grow up they leave their mother.

They fly away with other ducks.

Duck map

wings

beak

feathers

webbed feet

Glossary

 **beak** hard, pointed part of a bird's mouth

 **lay** when an egg comes out a mother animal's body

 **webbed feet** animal feet that have skin between the toes

 **wings** special arms covered in feathers that birds use to fly

Index